The Buzz About
Social Media

A Cyber Safety Workbook and Discussion Guide

for Pre-Teens, Ages 8 –12

D1509701

Shawn Marie Edgington

With Emily Scheinberg

Table of Contents

Introduction

This workbook has been put together for parents, educators, and children to bring about awareness on cyberbullying. Cyberbullying is affecting many youth around the world, and we are hoping that this resource will make readers more knowledgeable about cyberbullying and how to handle situations involving bullying.

The Buzz about Social Media was created to guide you through important discussions and activities related to cyber safety and proper online behavior. This workbook is filled with suggestions, real life situations and activities to help you discuss the best practices for cyber safety with your child. *The Buzz* was developed for you, and it should be customized by you, as you see fit.

We've combined practical information, proven suggestions, and need to know information to help you become knowledgeable with the most important cyber-safety issues that our children are facing today.

About The Author

Shawn Marie Edgington is a bestselling author and America's leading cyberbullying prevention expert. She's the author of the bestselling book, *The Parent's Guide To Texting, Facebook, and Social Media: Understanding the Benefits and Dangers of Parenting in a Digital World* and *Read Between The Lines: A Humorous Guide To Texting with Simplicity and Style*, the creator of the *One-Click Safety Series*, the founder of The Cyber Safety Academy, and the founder of The Great American NO BULL Challenge, as well as a change management speaker.

She is the CEO of a national insurance firm located in Northern California where she provides risk management and guidance to clients across the country about the repercussions of inappropriate social media and harassment usage in the workplace, among other business related exposures.

After a personal experience she had with her 16-year-old daughter being physically threatened by text and on Facebook, Shawn has made it her mission to provide parents with solutions that they can use to empower their children to defend against the threats they receive as a result of living in a digital world.

Shawn's developed the *One-Click Safety Kit*, a turnkey program filled with tools that help families defend against sexting, cyberbullies and textual harassment. She also developed *The Cyber Safety Academy Fundraiser,* filled with the highest quality safety products to help parents become cyber savvy.

Shawn and the NO BULL Team are always working on the only national video campaign for teens, Great American NO BULL Challenge. For more information, visit www.nobullchallenge.org.

Shawn has been profiled in the upcoming documentary *Submit: The Reality of Cyberbullying,* Fox Business, Imus in the Morning, View from the Bay, KRON 4 News, The San Francisco Chronicle, Fox News Radio, ESPN Radio, CBS Radio, The Leslie Marshall Show, InfoTrak, The John Carney Show, Mom's the Word, The San Diego Union, American Cheerleader Magazine, CNN Radio, NPR and various media outlets and syndicated radio programs across the country. Shawn joins Sharecare.com and Dr. Oz to provide her expertise to parents about cyber safety.

Shawn is working with Dr. Oz, Healthcorps and a team of experts as a health blogger for Teen Daily Strength, focusing on the life challenges that teens face related to cyberbullying, sexting, managing online reputations, and cyber safety. Teen Daily Strength (www.teendailystrength.com) is a new social networking website where teens can get information and ask questions anonymously.

Shawn continues to speak at conferences, school assemblies and meetings around the country to help shed light on the silent epidemic of textual harassment, cyberbullying and fatal Facebook mistakes parents can help their children avoid. Shawn is on a mission to help protect our kids against the silent epidemic of cyber-harassment, and wants every parent to get informed. If you're aware of what's happening, you can get involved and facilitate change. Shawn lives in the San Francisco Bay Area and is passionate about her family and helping others. To meet her or learn more about Ms. Edgington, you can visit her at www.shawnedgington.com

Mark Your Calendars

May 17th marks National Cyber Safety Awareness Day. On this day, parents and teachers alike should make an effort to incorporate a lesson on cyber safety. Without the help and direction of adults of appropriate usage in cyber space, children could make life-altering mistakes.

This resource will supply both adults and children with strategies on how to prevent cyberbullying, and also bring about an awareness of the cyberbullying that is currently taking place.

Much of the information comes from Shawn Edgington, bestselling author and cyberbullying prevention expert. Emily Scheinberg, a third grade teacher and a doctoral candidate at Indiana University of Pennsylvania, collaborated with Shawn on this project. In the near future, Emily plans to start her research for her dissertation, which will focus on parents' perspective on cyberbullying.

Cyberbullying Prevention

For centuries, parents have been able to easily protect and guard their children from bad people... but with today's technology, social networks and mobile messaging, it's simple for predators and bullies to reach out and attack our children from anywhere and at anytime, silently and with ease.

It's a fact that cyberbullying ruins lives. Cyberbullying occurs when a minor uses technology to deliberately and repeatedly engage in hostile behavior to harm or threaten another minor, and is against the law.

- ✓ Almost half of our youth experience some form of online harassment
- ✓ 71% of teens receive messages from strangers
- ✓ 39% of teenagers admit to sending or posting sexually suggestive messages (aka sexts)
- ✓ Most kids don't tell their parents what's happening in their online world

It's critical that parents take a pro-active approach and become aware of how technology can be abused and talk to their kids about the dos and don'ts for using technology. When it comes to cyberbullying, prevention is key:

- ✓ **Establish rules:** Be sure to sit down with your child to outline the rules of engagement for cell phone and Internet use, and have them agree to your rules by signing a contract.

- ✓ **Obey age restrictions:** Obey age limitations set by social networks. Facebook requires users to be at least 13-years-old.

- ✓ **Sexting and Internet avoidance:** If your child has a cell phone, make sure that it can't access the Internet. If their phone has a camera/video feature, contact your provider to disable their MMS service.

- ✓ **Invest in Parental Controls:** This service allows parents to "set text boundaries, disable text service after bedtime, and control who can be blocked from sending texts, among other benefits.

✓ **Check privacy and security settings, guard passwords:** Double check all of your child's security settings to be sure they are all set to private and instruct your child to <u>never</u> share their passwords with anyone.

✓ **Know your child's friends:** Frequently monitor whom your child is connected to. Be sure they are people that they know in real life, and people you trust.

✓ **Closely monitor Internet and cell phones:** Keep the computer in a visible place, and spot check text messages, videos and photos.

✓ **Think before posting:** Help your child manage their online image and reputation. Encourage your child to treat others online, as they want to be treated in real life. It's crucial they understand what's posted on the Internet stays on the Internet forever.

✓ **Limit Personal Information:** Be cautious about how much personal information your child posts. The more detailed the information, the easier it is for online predators, hackers, etc. to use their information to commit crimes.

✓ **Ignore/Block/Report:** Show your child how to ignore, block and report people who aren't being nice to them, whether in person, by text message or on the Internet. Help your child understand how important it is to <u>not</u> respond to any negative messages and to immediately report them to a trusted adult.

✓ **Contact the Authorities:** The police take cyberbullying very seriously. If your child is ever physically threatened or contacted by a stranger, notify the police immediately.

Children lack the maturity and experience to deal with a difficult situation like being the target of a cyberbully. Your child will look to you to help them respond appropriately and get through difficult situations. Knowledge is power! If you are aware of what's happening, you can get involved and facilitate change.

Resource Guide for
8 to 9-year-olds

Table of Contents

This section of the resource guide will help you identify what bullying and cyberbullying are, and what to do if you are involved in a bullying incident. The work that you complete in this workbook should be shared with an adult that you trust. Bullying will not stop unless you are open and honest about things that are happening in your life. If someone is bothering you at school or at home, make sure to tell a friend or another adult about it.

Things you can expect to learn about in this workbook:

Let's get started!

Draw a picture of what you think a bully looks like below:

Buzz Time 🐝

Directions: Take this quiz and then review the answers with your parent. If you don't understand one of the questions, ask for help.

| Yes | No | Is cyberbullying a big problem in your school? |

Yes No Is cyberbullying a big problem in your school?

Yes No Is spreading rumors a form of bullying?

Yes No Do boys bully?

Yes No I'm 11 and want a Facebook account. Is it legal for me to have one?

Yes No Is it okay to use my real name on my Facebook or MySpace account?

Yes No Does it help to answer back to a message that has lied about you to all your friends?

Yes No Is there any way to stop a person from cyberbullying you?

Yes No Do you have a friend that is being bullied?

Yes No Have you ever been bullied?

Yes No Would you tell your Mom or Dad if you were ever being cyberbullied?

Yes No Does your school have rules against cyberbullying and bullying?

Yes No Is name-calling a form of bullying?

Questions to Consider

- ✓ Do you know someone who is a bully, or who is being bullied?
- ✓ How does it make you feel when someone around you is being bullied?
- ✓ Do you think there is anything you can do about bullying?
- ✓ What does bullying mean?

A person is bullied when he or she is exposed to negative actions, repeatedly and over time, and has difficulty defending themselves.

Cyberbullying, as defined by the Centers for Disease Control, is: "any type of harassment or bullying (teasing, telling lies, making fun of someone, making rude or mean comments, spreading rumors, or making threatening or aggressive comments) that occurs through email, a chat room, instant messaging, a web site (including blogs), or text messaging."

Michael, age ten, was bullied at school nearly every day. Boys punched and kicked him on the playground (just out of sight from the teachers), stole his lunch money, and called him nasty names. Michael complained to his parents and the school nurse about stomach pains and headaches and often stayed home from school, but for months he said nothing about the bullying. What could Michael have done differently?

Answer:

Recognizing the Difference Between Bullying and Conflict

Examples of bullying:

 Excluding others

 Calling other's names

 Hitting

 Pushing

 Punching

 Having money taken from you

 Spreading rumors

 Being threatened or forced to do things

 Being bullied because of your race or religion

All of these can only be considered bullying if they are **REPEATED** over time.

Jenny, a new kindergarten student, had been looking forward to riding the school bus all summer, so her mother was puzzled when, after only a week, Jenny asked if her mom could drop her off at school instead. When her mother asked her why she didn't want to ride the bus anymore, Jenny admitted that some of the third-and-fourth grade girls on the bus had been taking her lunch each morning and calling her "baby."

Can you think of any examples of bullying that have taken place at school? Write them or draw a picture of them in the space below.

Bullying is Everywhere!

Take a minute and write down some of your favorite television shows.

Choose one of these shows, and watch it. As you watch it write down any behaviors that you think remind you of bullying.

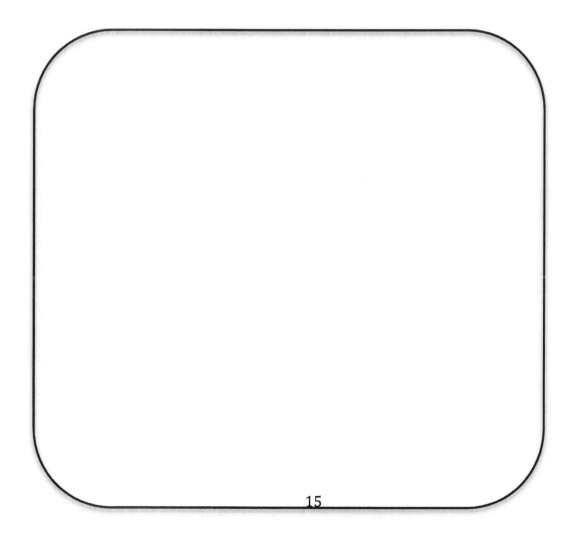

If you were a character in the show, how would you have handled the situation? Either draw a comic, or write about what you would do.

What can you encourage your friends to do when they see bullying taking place?

Appropriate Responses

If you do see bullying taking place at school or on the bus, you should immediately inform an adult. You should also do something about it. You would not want someone to walk away from you if you were being bullied.

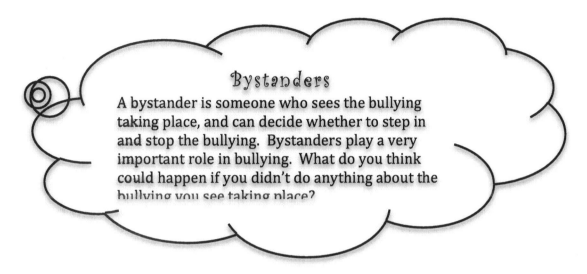

Bystanders
A bystander is someone who sees the bullying taking place, and can decide whether to step in and stop the bullying. Bystanders play a very important role in bullying. What do you think could happen if you didn't do anything about the bullying you see taking place?

Things that work when stepping in:

 Try changing the subject

 Make a joke that the bully is not expecting

 Find others who are around and have them stick up for the person who is getting bullied

 Make the person who is getting bullied feel like they did not deserve to be bullied.

 Don't back down! Sometimes bullies need challenged

Things you learned

Interesting things

Question you still have

What are Some Examples of Social Media?

- ✓ Cell Phones
- ✓ iTouch and MP3 Players
- ✓ Google Searches
- ✓ Facebook
- ✓ YouTube
- ✓ Online Gaming
- ✓ E-Mail

Guess How Many?

How many hours a day do children under the age of 18 spend using social media?

How many text messages does the average teenager send a month?

What's the number one thing teens spend their time doing while they are using social media?

How many users are on Facebook Worldwide?

How many are under the age of 13?

CYBER BULLYING

What is cyberbullying?

Cyberbullying is when a child uses technology as a weapon to intentionally threaten or hurt another child. The act of cyberbullying requires that the cyberbully *intends* to do harm or to torment their target.

**When you do something intentional, it means on purpose.

Ways that cyberbullies can attack:

 Text messages

 Phone calls

 Facebook, MySpace, and other social networking sites

 Pictures and Videos

 Instant Messaging

 E-mails

BEE Aware
If your online actions threaten, hurt, bother, or embarrass another person, you are being a cyber bully!

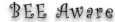

20

Cell Phones

Bullies use cell phones to attack their victims because then they don't have to look the person in the eye. They don't even have to talk to them if they don't want to.

Bullies typically send text messages, and say very mean and nasty things. Sometimes the bully also says something embarrassing in the text message, and sends it to many people at one time.

If you ever receive a text message that asks you something personal, or private, you should immediately tell an adult, even if it is embarrassing. You should not respond!

You can also block the sender of the inappropriate messages by having your parents use the parental controls that come with the phone plan. With the controls, parents can have certain things blocked from being sent to you.

Bullies sometimes send inappropriate pictures in text messages. This is called sexting. Sometimes, people may ask you for a picture, or may even take your picture, and send it out to others. It is very important for you to show this to an adult so that they can report it. No one has the right to make you feel uncomfortable.

You can protect yourself by **NEVER** agreeing to take an inappropriate picture or video of yourself.

It may seem embarrassing to show your parents an inappropriate picture of yourself. However, think of it this way—would you rather your parents see it first and get it removed, or everyone else in the world?! Even if it is embarrassing, you should never erase anything that is sent to you. With no evidence, it is difficult to find out who is bullying you.

What are some examples of how cyberbullying can happen to you?

- ✓ Someone can steal your password and pretend to be you
- ✓ They can embarrass, belittle, or harass you by text or on a social network
- ✓ Someone forwards a private message or photo that you sent

Reflect: Who would you go to first if someone asked you to send him or her an inappropriate picture?

_____

Who would you go to first if someone sent you an inappropriate picture? _____

Why is it important to not delete any pictures that are sent to you?

Phone Calls

Bullies also use the telephone to bully, or harass people. They may call your house, or cell phone many times, and hang up. They may prank call other people and say it is you. They may even call your house and say mean and nasty things about you and your family. If this happens you will want to report it to an adult.

Social Networking

People join social networks to socialize and find others with similar interests. Facebook is an example of a social networking Internet website. Its members have the ability to communicate with others in what is called real-time. This means that it is very close to talking to someone in person. Your friends can post you messages about anything, and anyone can see these messages.

Bullies may pretend to be your friend on a social networking site. They will want to find out about all of your secrets and embarrassing stories. After they have gained enough juicy information, they will post your embarrassing moments on the network for all of the other readers to enjoy.

You can prevent this from happening by not sharing personal information with others over the Internet. If these children are not your friends in school and other activities do you really think they will be your friends on the Internet?

Keep Private Things Private

It is very important to decide what gets put on the Internet and what does not. If your actions would make your parents disappointed, or make someone else feel bad, then you should not put the information online.

You should never allow anyone to pressure you into putting things on the Internet that you are uncomfortable with. You should also not put anything onto the Internet that could put you in danger. Remember to never give your full name, address, or where you go to school.

Fill in the chart with things that you think would be appropriate to put online for others to see, and what would be inappropriate.

Appropriate	Inappropriate

What would you do if someone tries to pressure you into putting inappropriate information online?

_____

_____

_____

Reflect: Do you belong to a social networking website?   **Y or N**

Have people that you don't know tried to be friends with you?   **Y or N**

Have you agreed to be friends with these strangers?   **Y or N**

What kinds of information do you share on the social networking site? Explain.

Making Responsible Choices

Staying Safe on Social Networks

- ✓ Set your settings to private
- ✓ Protect your passwords
- ✓ Remember the *Golden Rule Applies*
- ✓ Think before you post pictures, videos or statuses

Don't Connect with Strangers

- ✓ Protect your online image online & off
- ✓ Remember the Internet is permanent
- ✓ Remember the Internet is NOT private
- ✓ You never know whose watching
- ✓ Forwarding is easy and can often go viral, so don't send things you don't want going viral (public for everyone to see)
- ✓ Mistakes and consequences can be painful

Sharing Personal Information

Examples of things you should never place online, including on any social network like Facebook:

- ✓ Full Name
- ✓ Address
- ✓ Phone numbers
- ✓ Passwords
- ✓ School schedule
- ✓ School
- ✓ Location

Who Should Be Your Friend within a Social Network?

- ✓ Friends = Circle of Trust
- ✓ # of Friends in real life?
- ✓ How many are in your online circle?
- ✓ Watch out for too many "friends"

Watching out for Online Predators

- ✓ Predators try to meet kids online, so they can harm them in real life
- ✓ Predators try to get you to trust them online
- ✓ Predators send gifts
- ✓ Predators turn you against your family and friends
- ✓ Predators talk about uncomfortable topics or share revealing pictures
- ✓ Predators make you feel guilty or ashamed

—My friend received a friend request on Facebook from a cute boy who said he went to the other middle school in our city. My friend accepted his request, and it turned out he was really a 52-year-old man who was trying to take advantage of my friend.

Predator Avoidance

- ✓ Don't accept FRIEND requests from people you don't know
- ✓ If you find out you have a stranger in your network, BLOCK them immediately
- ✓ You have the power to avoid them

Social Network Rules to Live By

Before signing up for any social networking site, you should follow these 10 important rules to live by. After reading each rule, write down why you think it is an important rule to follow.

Your parents can and will request your password so they can monitor your online social content and postings on a regular basis. Ask them to teach you how to safeguard, or protect, your password. Be prepared for your parents to explain how important it is to NEVER tell anyone your password, not even your best friend.

_____

_____

Expect your parents to teach you how to use the "Block" and "Report" feature to stop any type of offensive or abusive behavior.
   IGNORE - DON'T RESPOND & make a copy of the message if you feel it's necessary
   BLOCK - Call your wireless provider or go online to have the number blocked
   REPORT - Report the harassment to parents and the police when necessary

_____

_____

Know that the pages on your social networking site will be frequently monitored. Your parents will watch for photos, posts, bullies, and anything that doesn't seem right. They will also watch for "tagging" and photos that have been posted to your profile.

_____

_____

Make sure that your accounts are always set on "Private" and make sure to avoid posting private information, especially information that could lead to a physical attack. (Example: address, phone number, etc. should not be posted).

_____

_____

Watch out for foul or inappropriate language – delete posts or updates that include this type of language.

_____

_____

Watch out for inappropriate photo posts – think twice before posting updates and delete inappropriate photos immediately.

_____

_____

Only accept friend requests from people you know. Expect that your parents will frequently review your friends list, keeping an eye open for people they don't know.

_____

_____

"Checking in" or updating a post using Facebook Places is dangerous and off limits.

_____

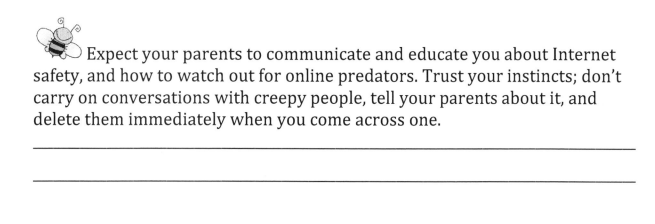 Expect your parents to communicate and educate you about Internet safety, and how to watch out for online predators. Trust your instincts; don't carry on conversations with creepy people, tell your parents about it, and delete them immediately when you come across one.

 Read over the "Rules of Engagement" with your parents.

Important: For children between the ages of 8-14, take a look at the new social network imbee. It's a cool, safe and fun environment for teens to share their social experiences online. www.imbee.com

The Buzz About the Internet

When you share things over the Internet, they can never be erased. Even though you may be young now, those things can always come back to haunt you.

Because so many people have access to the Internet and technology, it is difficult to escape what is being said through social media.

Two important things to keep in mind:

THINK BEFORE YOU CLICK

BECAUSE

The Whole World is Watching

Who's Watching?

- ✓ Coaches
- ✓ Teachers
- ✓ Your Administrators
- ✓ Your Parents
- ✓ Other Parents
- ✓ Potential Employers
- ✓ The Police

Roles in Bullying Situations

When bullying takes place, there are different roles that are filled. There is usually a queen bee, bystanders, and the victim of bullying.

- ✓ Usually starts the bullying
- ✓ Gets others to engage in bullying incidents
- ✓ Pretends to be your friend, and then stings you
- ✓ Has an audience
- ✓ May have been bullied at some point, and wants to get back at others
- ✓ Is very polite around parents, so parents have a hard time believing they are a bully

There are different types of bystanders. Some allow bullying to continue and other intervene and get the bully to stop.

- ✓ Turn the other way when bullying is taking place, so the action continues
- ✓ Cheer on the bully, so bullying continues to take place
- ✓ Intervene and help the victim, so that the bullying will stop
- ✓ Sometimes are afraid to say something because they don't want to be the next target

✓ Selected at random, if the bully is bored
✓ Can be targeted because of race, religion, clothing, language
✓ Suffers from embarrassment
✓ Does not want to come to school
✓ Feel lonely

When technology is used to bully:

✓ Children gang up on their target by sending thousands of text messages to their victim's mobile device, resulting in what is called a "text attack"
✓ A child can create a screen name that is similar to the victim's name and post inappropriate things to other users that the victim never said, which causes drama and trouble.
✓ Children can steal passwords of their victims and then lock the victim out of his or her own account
✓ Children will verbally abuse another child who is playing an online game with them
✓ Children recruit others to do their dirty work for them. These accomplices are the ones to get in trouble if they are caught.

FRiENdS RoCK!

The Golden Rule: Treat others the way you wish to be treated

I am sure you have heard this saying a million times. It is very important to think about the golden rule as you join a social network and make new friends. You do not want to forget about the friends you already have. The following tips will assist you in making sure that the Golden Rule is followed. It is totally okay to have more than one group of friends. These different groups will reflect the different interests that you have.

 Invite others to play along with you and your friends.

 Don't take your anger out on someone else. Find positive things to be happy about.

 Get involved with a variety of activities, so that you can meet people from different backgrounds. You will find that you have more in common than you think.

 Encourage your friends to befriend someone new. It's always nice to add new friends to the circle.

 Learn about the cultural differences of children in your classroom. You can learn a lot just by listening.

How Can I Have Fun and Make Sure No One is Left Out?

Imbee.com is a new social networking site created for kids just like you!! Here, you can meet up with your friends, share the latest news, upload appropriate photos and videos, watch shows, download music, buy things, and meet new people. Your parents wouldn't even have to worry because this networking site is made for tweens!!! Meaning...it is a safe environment!

Social networking is a great way to keep all of your friends involved without making anyone feel left out. By "friending" the friends you already have in school, or on a sports team you know that it is safe to chat with them through imbee.

Why such a goofy name?

The name imbee came from thinking that this networking site is for those "in between" kids who just aren't quite old enough for Facebook, and are too young for other things such as Club Penguin.

Is it easy to set-up an account?

It's simple: kids register with the help of their parents and the parents set the controls for the kid's site experience.

Is there a fee?

Imbee is free, however there is a one-time fee of $1 to ensure that you have your parent's permission and also to prove that your address is correct. If you want access to the premium package, it costs $7.99, but many awesome features are offered for free!

The Friends Rock Campaign

What is it?

- ✓ The "FRIENDS ROCK" Campaign is a joint effort between parents, schools, and communities to prevent bullying from taking place, while teaching the importance of true friendship.

- ✓ Each party should work hard to promote awareness about bullying by discussing what it means to be a true friend.

How Can I get involved?

- ✓ Start a revolution or a cause in your school, organization, or community with awareness "FRIENDS ROCK" silicon bracelets that promote no bullying in a cool way. These wristbands can be found inside of the Cyber Safety Academy Fundraiser. For more information, go to www.cybersafetyacademy.com

- ✓ Start a cyber safety fundraiser in your school or organization to raise funds and awareness. Go to www.cybersafetyacademy.com to find out how.

Why is it important?

- ✓ Not everyone is aware of the cyberbullying problem that exists in our schools, and what defines an act of cyberbullying.

- ✓ Children will take an active role in the campaign in order to facilitate change.

- ✓ Unless your child has been bullied or cyberbullied, you may think that it can't or won't happen in your family. As you read on, you will find out troubling statistics that prove otherwise.

When it comes to your cyber savvyness it's important to understand the Dos and Don'ts...

Dos	Don'ts
✓ Treat others respectfully	✓ Target others because you are feeling bad about yourself
✓ Tell a trusted adult if you or someone else is being bullied	✓ Keep bullying incidents to yourself
✓ Learn appropriate ways to use technology	✓ Use technology in ways that you know will put you or someone else at risk
✓ Find age appropriate activities to do with technology	✓ Do something just because someone else told you to

Don't allow others to **BUG** you while you're on the computer.

Things you can to prevent this from happening:

 Don't give out your passwords

Work with your parents to set up appropriate guidelines to keep you safe while using the Internet and other forms of technology

Get creative with your friends. Have contests to design informational brochures about Internet safety. Share your brochures with your classmates, school, and local libraries.

If you feel uncomfortable in a situation, remove yourself. You do not have to give a reason for excusing yourself.

You are not being a tattletale if you are trying to keep a friend safe. If someone you, or someone you know is in danger, it is best to inform an adult.

Share what you know with others. If they see how much fun technology can be, they will want to participate also.

Want to make a promise to yourself (or your parents) to be cyber savvy?

The Promise

✓ I promise I will never join in or laugh if I see or hear someone is being bullied.
✓ I promise if someone is being bullied in person or using technology, I won't stand by and do nothing.
✓ I promise I will tell a teacher, a parent, an adult or a trusted friend if I become aware of anyone who is a target of a bully or a cyberbully.
✓ I promise I will not respond to any bullying message or image, and I will make a copy of the evidence, and then delete it.
✓ I promise I will never forward an image of someone else, no matter what.

My Name:

Things you learned

Interesting things

Question you still have

Find the words below:

```
E N S F E W I L S F G E C T F
R L O M I N A U W R S Y C N L
N E A I S L O I B I B T K E A
D I T T S M T L N E H E O M M
L I A U Y S O E R N B X O S I
M N G N P C E B R D E T B S N
T R O I K M U R E I W I E A G
Q N A I T L O A G N N N C R Y
A I N H L A H C Y G R G A A T
N G Y Y G O L B V E A U F H X
G N I P P A L S Y P P A H P Y
M N E F F T C E L L P H O N E
G N I Y L L U B E C A P S Y M
I N T E R N E T W O R K L N B
E L I F O R P R E V E N G E V
```

AGGRESSION ANONYMOUS BLOCKING BLOG BULLYING
CELLPHONE COMPUTER CYBERBULLYING DIGITAL EMAIL
FACEBOOK FILTERING FLAMING FRIENDING HAPPY
SLAPPING HARASSMENT HARM INSTANT INTERNET
MYSPACE NETWORK PROFILE REVENGE TEXTING WEB

Tool Kit for Parents & Educators of 8 to 9-year-olds

Communication is Key

Bullying is a growing problem in schools across the country, but because of widespread access to technology, bullying does not stop there. Children now torment others from the comfort of their own homes through technological devices including the computer and cell phones.

Consider This:
How many 8 and 9 year olds do you know that have their own cell phones, email addresses, and access to the Internet? How many of these same children interact with your own child on a daily basis?

List reasons why access to technology may be beneficial to children whom are 8-9 years old:

Do these benefits outweigh the dangers that are associated with access to these forms of technology?

Think Happy Thoughts

Having access to technology can be a very positive experience for young children if they are taught how to navigate social network sites and the Internet, and are taught how to use technology appropriately. Just like in school, there is nothing wrong with having an acceptable usage policy in place at home. However, as a parent, you should really take the time to explain what acceptable use means. Especially at 8 and 9 years of age, children need modeling to truly understand what you are explaining to them.

Have meaningful conversations with your child about why they shouldn't share personal information with strangers on the computer, belong to a social network that's not age appropriate, or use their cell phone to hurt others or send inappropriate images or texts.

Many children, even at 8 and 9 years old, are fearful of telling their parents that something has taken place on the Internet or by text because they don't want their privileges taken away. It is important for your child to know that you are on their side, and that when something occurs that they are uncomfortable with, you are there for them to talk to. Explain to them that you would rather them be honest about anything that occurs in this "digital playground" because you are looking out for their best interest. It is very easy to be naïve about things, but when dealing with the Internet and mobile devices, it is better to be proactive instead of reactive.

Set up guidelines together with your child. You will want to develop a contract that both parties agree with. In addition, it wouldn't hurt to set up a procedure for reporting any negative actions that take place on the Internet. Because there is so much cyberbullying being reported on the news across the country, it could be a great conversation starter. Things such as- "I saw this on the news last night. Have you heard of these things before?" or "Someone at work told me about something really awful that happened to one of their children's friends. Do things like this happen with your friends?" If your children know that you are willing to be open with them about the issues taking place on the Internet, and that you are not passing judgment on others, they will be more likely to admit when bullying and cyberbullying are taking place and affecting them.

Ways to Encourage Safe Use of Technology

imbee
- Social Networking
- Age appropriate

Cell Phones
- Phone should be charged in the parent's bedroom
- Activate parental controls from Service Provider
- Parents should disable the MMS feature

Skype
- Child should only talk to family members
- Should be supervised when using this application

Gaming (Wii, PlayStation, Xbox Live)
- Parent should be aware of what games are played
- Parent should have access to password
- Child should be supervised while playing

Emails
- Child should always be supervised when emailing friends
- Parent should have access to password

Your Input
- A:
- B:

How will parents feel about their children being on a social network at a young age?

imbee is focused on a very specific demographic that has largely been ignored. Most of the kid's sites focus on very young kids or they aren't really for kids at all, but for their parents. That's where imbee comes in. We are focused on providing cool and interesting content and talent that reflect the demographic the fast-paced, edgy world kids live in today. imbee has managed to harness all of the incredible social media offerings available and package them in one safe place.

You can learn more about imbee at www.imbee.com

Facts About imbee that you will appreciate:

imbee has premium security settings and is COPPA compliant

The built-in security settings allow kids and their parents to decide how much or how little can be seen on the site

Without parent authorization, kids won't have full access to the site

The site is monitored 24/7 and crawlers are also used to detect breaches of site conduct and inappropriate contact

There are guidelines in place for site misconduct: first the user is directly contacted, second the parents are contacted, and finally if needed, the user is blocked from the site.

imbee's goal is to work with parents and their children so they can talk about what is on the site and collaborate on site usage.

Resource Guide for 10 to 12-year-olds

Table of Contents:

This workbook is meant to serve as a communication tool between you, your parents, or your schoolteacher. Sometimes, you may feel that you are alone, but after reading this workbook and completing the activities, you will see that you are not alone!

You will also find strategies that you can utilize to stop bullying from occurring. Be honest as you complete the activities. By being honest, you will be able to find the help and resources that you need to take an active role in preventing cyberbullying.

Keep in mind that you are not alone, and that adults are available for your support. Sometimes, they are not as knowledgeable as you would like them to be, so be patient, and explain to them exactly what is going on.

Things can expect to find in this workbook:

Social Networking Facts

What is Cyberbullying?

Keep Private Things Private

Privacy, Safety, and Security Online

Managing your Online Image and Reputation

Sext Education

Online Responsibility

Dos and Don'ts

The Pledge

Conclusions and Take Away's

Parent Tool Kit

Since most kids don't worry too much about what they say or do online, I've decided to share a very personal story with you, in hopes that it helps you understand the importance of cyber safety for yourself.

But first, let me give you a few important statistics:

- ✓ Recent studies show that almost 50% of teenagers have been harassed online.
- ✓ And that almost 40% of teens have admitted to sexting.
- ✓ 71% of our children receive messages from strangers online, and 30% of those children *think about* meeting those strangers face- to- face.

I know what you might be thinking; these statistics don't apply to me. But I want you to know that they do, because my daughter became one of those statistics.

Two years ago, my daughter, a straight "A" student, a student body officer, a cheerleader, and a girl that had fifty best friends, ended up being targeted by a group of bullies who stalked her, harassed her, and physically threatened her with thousands of text messages and Facebook posts.

As a result of my daughter being cyberbullied, her entire personality and behavior changed, and to this day, she is not the same girl that she used to be. Here's what happened:

- ✓ She completely shut her friends out of her life, and refused to go anywhere or do anything
- ✓ She lost trust in the people that she was closest with
- ✓ In college, she still has a hard time opening herself up to new situations and friendships

My daughter taught me that when people say cruel things over and over again about you, that eventually you start to believe what they are saying is true, even though it couldn't be farther from the truth. She also taught me that being threatened on a social network is like being singled out and placed on the world's stage for everyone to watch and join in on the slander.

I manage risk, specialize in safety, and prevent loss for a living, but I didn't know where to begin when it came to protecting my daughter from cyberbullies.   If I only knew then what I know now, I could have saved my daughter from the heartache and psychological warfare that she still struggles to overcome today.

When I found out that millions of kids are affected every year by online harassment, I knew I wouldn't be doing my fellow parents a service by keeping my personal experience and outcomes a secret. It's the reason I wrote my latest book: ***The Parent's Guide to Texting, Facebook and Social Media: Understanding the Benefits and Dangers of Parenting in a Digital World***, which recently became a bestseller.

It's my personal mission to provide every child and parent with awareness, solutions, and preventative resources to keep their children safe and secure while they're online.

With defensive actions and constant communication with our teens, we can teach you about the potential dangers of social networking, empower you to protect themselves from online predators, guard your personal information, preserve your online reputation, and learn how to determine friends from "frenemies."

The truth is, knowledge is power! If you are aware of what's happening, you can get involved and facilitate change.

For Parents & Educators:

This section of the workbook was created for 10-12 year olds. While the book can be completed independently, it is wise for an adult (parent or teacher) to supervise the work that is being completed. Without communicating about the information that is recorded in the workbook, very little can be done to cease bullying. In order to prevent bullying from occurring, and stop it if it has already started, both adults and children need to work collaboratively.

This workbook serves as a communication tool between adults and children. Questions should be thought about, and answered as honestly as possible.

Within this workbook, you can expect to find many valuable resources. The sections that can be located in the workbook include:

- ✓ Social Networking Facts
- ✓ What is Cyberbullying?
- ✓ Keep Private Things Private
- ✓ Privacy, Safety, and Security Online
- ✓ Managing Your Online Image and Reputation
- ✓ Sext Education
- ✓ Online Responsibility
- ✓ Do's and Don'ts
- ✓ The Pledge
- ✓ Conclusions and Take Away's
- ✓ Parent Tool Kit

Online Dangers

Being connected to the digital world is something that isn't going away anytime soon! Having access to technology is just one more way for children and adult predators to target their prey. It's disturbing to know that:

- ✓ About half of all teenagers have experienced some form of online harassment (Cyberbullying Research Center).
- ✓ 37 percent of teens admit to using social networking sites to victimize and harass their peers (TheExaminer.com).
- ✓ 43 percent of teens use their cell phones to say insulting things to others (LG Mobile Phones).
- ✓ 64 percent of all teens say they do things online they don't want their parents to know about (Lenhart, Madden, Rainie, 2006).
- ✓ 71 percent of teens receive messages online from strangers (National Center for Missing and Exploited Children).
- ✓ 51 percent of teens have been asked for personal information online (McAfee Inc.)
- ✓ 83 percent of teens admit to texting in the middle of the night (LG Mobile Phones).
- ✓ 45 percent of teens admit to texting and driving (LG Mobile Phones).
- ✓ 30 percent of teens contemplate meeting a person they met online (Teenage Research Unlimited).
- ✓ 42 percent of youth, age ten to seventeen, have seen Internet porn in the past year. Two-thirds of these exposures were unwanted (University of New Hampshire's Crimes Against Children Research Center).

CYBER BULLYING

Cyberbullying affects more individuals than you think. A survey conducted amongst 4th through 8th graders found that:

🐝 58 percent of kids report that someone has been hurtful or mean to them online

🐝 21 percent of kids claim that they have received threatening messages, either by text messaging or through social media accounts

🐝 35 percent of kids say that they have received threats online

🐝 42 percent of kids classify mean behavior towards them online as bullying

🐝 53 percent of kids admit that they have said something mean to someone else online

Survey results were taken from the i-SAFE survey located on
http://www.troubledteen101.com/articles61.html

Definition of Cyberbullying

Cyberbullying is when a minor uses technology as a weapon to intentionally threaten or hurt another minor. The act of cyberbullying requires that the cyberbully *intends* to do harm or to torment their target.

Why Cyberbullying is Hard to Understand?

It is difficult for parents to understand cyberbullying because chances are when they were younger; bullies just harassed them on the schoolyard, bus, or in the hallways.

They don't fully recognize that bullies now have the means to harass you twenty-four hours a day, seven days a week! It is hard for anyone really to understand, unless you have been a victim of cyberbullying. There are many types of cyberbullying, including:

 Sending mean messages to a person

 Spreading rumors or lies about someone online

 Excluding someone from online conversations

 Creating a website or a page to make fun of someone

 Threatening or harassing someone online or by text

 Tricking someone into sharing secrets and then spreading that information around online or by text

 Breaking into someone else's account, stealing their password, and using their account to send mean or hurtful messages, pretending you are them

 Taking pictures or videos of a person and sharing them without the person's consent

Brief Description of the Types of Cyberbullying

Denigration

- Spreading information about someone that is mean and untrue
- An example would be hurtful information that's been posted on a social network like FaceBook

Flaming

- When there is a brief argument between 2 more individuals
- Usually takes place on a social network

Harassment

- When one individual attacks another using a social network, text messages, or phones

Outing

- When you share personal, embarassing information with others about someone else on a social network or by text

Trickery

- When you trick someone into revealing personal information about themselves
- Then you use the information against them on a social network or by text

Happy Slapping

- When someone walks up and slaps someone else, while another individual captures the violence on a cell phone
- The video is then sent out to everyone you have as a contact

 Quiz Time

Directions: Have your child answer these questions as best they can. Review the answers together.

1. What do you find most appealing about the computer and/or cell phone?

2. About how many of your friends have cell phones, belong to a social network like Facebook, or have their own email addresses?

3. If you or one of your friends was cyberbullied, what would you do?

4. Would you tell a friend?

5. Would you tell an adult?

6. In your opinion, how does cyberbullying differ from traditional bullying?

7. If you could teach your parents about one thing you do on the computer, what would it be?

8. Do you believe your parents know how you use the Internet?

9. Do your parents call you or text you?

10. Which would you prefer they do, text you or call you?

11. Do you believe that your parents should have access to your passwords?

Interest Survey

In school, you have probably taken interest surveys at the beginning of the year. The purpose of them is to give an adult an idea of what your interests are, so that they can make learning experiences more meaningful for you. Parents also need some guidance on what makes you happy! Answer the following questions honestly!

1. When I go to a friend's house, we spend most of our time:

   ____ Playing video games (X-box, Wii, Play Station, etc.)

   ____ Riding bikes

   ____ Playing on the computer (updating profiles, playing online games, instant messaging, or talking in chat rooms)

   ____ Other

2. When I get home from school, the first thing I want to do is:

   _____

3. Place a check next to your preference:

   ____ I prefer playing games online against people I have never met

   ____ I prefer playing games in person with my friends or family as opponents (Wii, Play Station, X-box)

4. Place a check next to you preference:

   ____ I would consider myself outgoing and can strike up a conversation with anyone

   ____ I prefer talking to people online when I don't have to see them face-to-face

5. Place a check next to the technology applications that you have used in the last year:

_____ Facebook

_____ Text messaging

_____ Other Social networks like YouTube and imbee

_____ Posted pictures online

_____ E-mails

_____ Gaming (like World of Warcraft)

6. Who taught you how to use these applications?

_____ Teacher

_____ Friend

_____ Parent/Guardian

_____ Sibling

_____ Friend's parent

_____ Your own exploration

7. In the last year have you posted anything online that you wish you wouldn't have? What was it?

8. Did your parents discuss the do's and don'ts with you when you're online or using your cell phone?

These answers should be shared with your parents so that they can have a better understanding of what you like to do in your free time

What's posted on the Internet stays On the Internet forever!

Consider This:

Once something is posted online you cannot take it back. Even if you meant it as a joke, someone else may not find it very funny. People can be very sensitive about certain things, and you have to remember that once something is posted online millions of people have access to it. You should always

THINK BEFORE YOU CLICK

BECAUSE

The Whole World Is Watching

Who's Watching?

- ✓ Coaches
- ✓ Teachers
- ✓ Your Administrators
- ✓ Your Parents
- ✓ Other Parents
- ✓ Potential Employers
- ✓ The Police

To Share or NOT to Share?

If your best friend asked you for your password would you give it them? Read on to find out why that may not be such a great idea.

Passwords are created so that only certain people have access to things. If you wanted everything to be public information then why did you create a password in the first place? It is natural to always want to know what is going on with other people, but there is a difference between being curious and being sneaky.

Spying would be considered being sneaky. If you sneak peeks at your friends texts without permission, check out someone's call history, or even look at your friend's inbox of texts, you are being sneaky, or spying.

Passwords are set up as a precaution. Your parents should have access to them as a safety measure, but sharing them with your friends could lead to problems. Friends always have disagreements. What would happen if you were having a disagreement, and one of your friends chooses to share your password with others? Even if it is your best friend asking for your password, you should always so no, and say that no one has access to your password.

In addition to not sharing your password with people you know there are things you should NEVER share with people you have just met on the Internet.

Your real name

Your address

Your phone number

Name of your school

Your photo

You never know who is hiding behind a picture! That is why you should not share your personal information!

Sometimes the person hiding behind the picture is up to no good. These people are called predators. They prey on young adults and kids, so they can harm them in real life.

Ways Predators will try to get you to trust them online

- ✓ Send gifts
- ✓ Turn you against your family and friends
- ✓ Talk about uncomfortable topics or share revealing pictures
- ✓ Make you feel guilty or ashamed
- ✓ Remember: you have the power to avoid them!

Some precautions you can take to avoid predators:

- ✓ Don't accept them
- ✓ Block them
- ✓ Tell someone if they try to contact you
- ✓ NEVER agree to meet them

Think about it:

My friend was approached by a stranger who figured out where she went to school and what time her practice was from a picture she posted of herself playing soccer at school.

Advice for Setting up a Good Password

By mixing up your passwords with numbers and upper and lowercase letters, it will make it more difficult for someone to try and figure out what your password is. You want to trick others, but don't choose passwords that are so difficult, that even you can't figure out or remember what they are!

Do's	Don'ts
✓ Pick 2 favorite colors (redblue) ✓ Use numbers and letters together (1red2blue) ✓ Mix upper and lowercase letters (1Red2Blue)	✓ Choose your birthday, your name, your pet's name, or your brother or sister's name ✓ Give your password to anyone but a parent or guardian

How Do You Use Social Media?

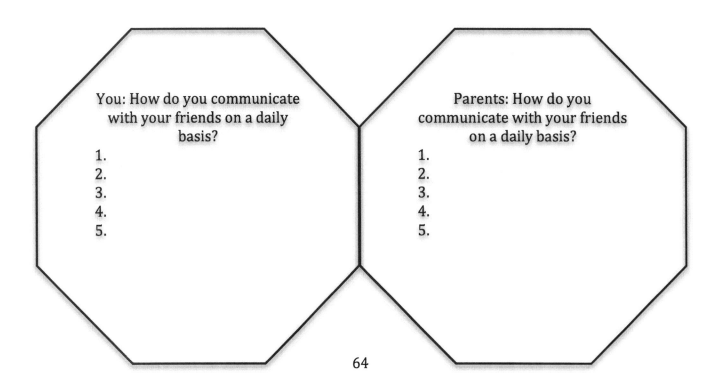

You: How do you communicate with your friends on a daily basis?
1.
2.
3.
4.
5.

Parents: How do you communicate with your friends on a daily basis?
1.
2.
3.
4.
5.

Did you and your parents have similar answers? Chances are that you don't! Parents and children interact differently. I am sure if you ask your parents what they use technology for and how, their answers will also appear to be different than yours. Let's find out.

You: What are the main things that you use technology for?

1.

2.

3.

4.

5.

6.

Your Parents: What are the main things that you use technology for?

1.

2.

3.

4.

5.

6.

How Important is technology to you and your parents?

What technology could you not live without?

In your opinion, what technology could your parents not live without?

Now it's your parent's turn!

What technology could you not live without?	What technology could your child not live without?

Did your answers match up? As you can see, parents and children use technology for different reasons and that is okay! However, parents should be aware of the applications that their children are using. It wouldn't hurt to learn something new from your child!

Parents need to realize that their children are connected to others through technology. Technology is how children communicate with others 24/7. So the worst thing you can say to your child if they report that they have been cyberbullied is to tell them not to go on the computer anymore or take their cell phone away.

These are the worst responses because not only has your child been victimized, but also now you are taking them away from their social connections that are very important to them. This seems like another punishment for something that isn't their fault. This is one of the main reasons children do not report cyberbullying—they don't want to be taken out of communication! Keep this in mind if your child reports cyberbullying to you. In addition, taking technology away from your child may result in a lack of trust. There are other ways to deal with the situation.

SEXTING

Sounds silly, but it is actually very serious

What's the big deal?

At this age, you are probably not really thinking about the future- college or having a job. When you get involved with sexting though, you are putting yourself at risk of never having to think about those things. Getting involved with sexting can negatively impact your life forever.

Sexting is sending or forwarding nude, sexually suggestive, or explicit messages, pictures, or video from your cell or online. For some people, it's no big deal. But real problems can happen when the parties involved are under 18 are pressured into sexting, and when sexts go viral.

> ### You should always have your future in mind.
>
> Colleges and employers are now checking Facebook, MySpace and other social media sites to see what kind of person you are - not just how popular you are and how many sports you participated in, but to see if you've ever been involved in any sexting situations. If you have, they may decide to take another applicant over you.

67

Questions you should stop and ask yourself:

Who's idea was this?

- You should never feel pressured to take pictures of yourself that expose your body
- If you are embarassed, and don't want to take the picture or video, don't!

Do you know where these pictures could end up?

- You may be in a relationship now, but what happens when it ends?
- With one click, these pics and videos can be sent to anyone and everyone!
- They can end up on FaceBook or posted on YouTube in seconds.

Have you thought of the consequences?

- Your reputation could be destroyed
- You could be arrested for sending the pictures
- You might have to register as a sex offender

Problems Associated with Sexting

- ✓ Potential to be arrested and charged for child pornography
- ✓ Requirement to register as a sex offender
- ✓ Humiliation among peers because a once-private photo was posted online and/or forwarded to others
- ✓ Injuries, suicides, and attacks can be the end result
- ✓ Attraction of stalkers/online predators
- ✓ Hazing/name-calling
- ✓ Sexual harassment, textual harassment, or sextortion
- ✓ Possible expulsion from school

You never know where the photo will end up, so don't take a picture that you will regret later.

Don't sext if you don't want to; you will feel much better about your self in the long run.

Points of Interest

Never forward a sext, break the cycle; you would want someone to break it if it was your picture?

If you never take a nude photo, how is it going to end up on the Internet?

Always Think Before you Click

- ✓ Assume a webcam is always on.

- ✓ Nothing that is said or done online is private.

- ✓ What's posted on the Internet stays on the Internet forever.

- ✓ Videos and pictures cannot be deleted once they are posted.

- ✓ School admissions officers, coaches, friends, and potential employers are using Facebook as part of their background checking process.

- ✓ Your image is worth protecting.

Social Network Rules to Live By

Before signing up for any social networking site, you should follow these 10 important rules to live by. After reading each rule, write down why you think it is an important rule to follow.

Your parents can and will request your password so they can monitor your online social content and postings on a regular basis. Ask them to teach you how to safeguard, or protect, your password. Be prepared for your parents to explain how important it is to NEVER tell anyone your password, not even your best friend.

_____

_____

Expect your parents to teach you how to use the "Block" and "Report" feature to stop any type of offensive or abusive behavior.

IGNORE - DON'T RESPOND & make a copy of the message if you feel it's necessary
BLOCK - Call your wireless provider or go online to have the number blocked
REPORT - Report the harassment to parents and the police when necessary

_____

_____

Know that the pages on your social networking site will be frequently monitored. Your parents will watch for photos, posts, bullies, and anything that doesn't seem right. They will also watch for "tagging" and photos that have been posted to your profile.

_____

_____

Make sure that your accounts are always set on "Private" and make sure to avoid posting private information, especially information that could lead to a physical attack. (Example: address, phone number, etc. should not be posted).

_____

_____

Watch out for foul or inappropriate language – delete posts or updates that include this type of language.

_____

_____

Watch out for inappropriate photo posts – think twice before posting updates and delete inappropriate photos immediately.

_____

_____

Only accept friend requests from people you know. Expect that your parents will frequently review your friends list, keeping an eye open for people they don't know.

_____

_____

"Checking in" or updating a post using Facebook Places is dangerous and off limits.

_____

_____

Expect your parents to communicate and educate you about Internet safety, and how to watch out for online predators. Trust your instincts; don't carry on conversations with creepy people, tell your parents about it, and delete them immediately when you come across one.

_____

_____

Read over the "Rules of Engagement" with your parents.

_____

_____

Important: For children between the ages of 8-14, take a look at the new social network imbee. It's a cool, safe and fun environment for teens to share their social experiences online. www.imbee.com

What Would You Do?

Two female sixth graders, Katie and Sarah, are exchanging malicious instant messages back and forth because of a misunderstanding involving a boy named Jacob. The statements escalate from trivial name-calling to very vicious and inflammatory statements, including death threats.

Should the police be contacted? Are both girls wrong? What should the kids do in this instance?

A mother is walking by her son Jonathan while he is on the computer and notices that he keeps hiding the screen when she walks by. Upon further observation, the mother sees that Jonathan is making fun of someone else via instant messaging.

What should the mother do first? Does the mother need to contact the parents of the other child? Should Jonathan be allowed to use the computer?

What would you do?

If you were threatened by text message or harassed or made fun of on a social network?

If your friend was being made fun of online or by text?

If you received a friend request from someone you didn't know in real life?

If you received an inappropriate text message in order to forward it out to everyone?

With so many limitations, it probably seems like there is nothing fun for you to do on the Internet. You probably feel like even if you were involved with a social network, that your mom and dad would be constantly looking over your shoulder. However, help is on the way! There is something designed totally for you!

What is there for me?

imbee is a new social networking site created for kids just like you!! Here, you can meet up with your friends, share the latest news, upload appropriate photos and videos, watch shows, download music, buy things, and meet new people. Your parents wouldn't even have to worry because this networking site is made for kids ages 8-14! Meaning, this is a safe environment!

Why such a goofy name?

The name imbee came from thinking that this networking site is for those "in between" kids who just aren't quite old enough for Facebook, and are too young for other things such as Club Penguin.

Is it easy to get an account?

It's simple: kids register with the help of their parents and the parents set the controls for the kid's site experience.

How will my parents feel about imbee?

imbee is focused on a very specific demographic that has largely been ignored. Most of the kid's sites focus on very young kids or they aren't really for kids at all, but for their parents. That's where imbee comes in. We are focused on providing cool and interesting content and talent that reflect that demographic and the fast-paced and edgy world kids live in today. Imbee has managed to harness all of the incredible social media offerings available and package them in one safe place.

Campaign

What is the "NO BULL" Campaign?
✓ The "NO BULL" Campaign is movement to stop cyberbullying. The campaign is a joint effort between parents, schools, and communities to prevent bullying from taking place.
✓ Each party should work hard to promote awareness about bullying.

How can you get involved?
✓ To start a NO BULL movement in your school and for more information on how you can win big, visit www.nobullchallenge.org
✓ You can wear bracelets or lanyards that support the cause. To locate NO BULL awareness items, go to www.teamnobull.org
✓ Start a cyber safety fundraiser in your school or organization to raise funds and awareness. Go to www.cybersafetyacademy.com to find out how.
✓ You can inform others (both adults and your peers) about cyberbullying
✓ You can raise money for your school to bring in a bullying expert to speak to your school.
✓ If you witness cyberbullying, you can take the initiative to report it.

Why is it important?
✓ Adults need children to spread the word about worthwhile causes
✓ With your help, many more people will become aware of what cyberbullying is and how it can be prevented
✓ Your community and school will become a much safer place!

In the End...
Bullying will only stop if each and every person does his or her part to not participate in bullying. It is difficult at times to stand up for the right thing, but it only takes one person.

The person that you protect from being bullied will be forever grateful to you. In addition, you will become a role model for others. They will see that they too can stand up for what is right.

Be your own "Queen Bee" and set a positive example for others by not letting bullying and cyberbullying sting you or others that you care about.

Think about these numbers
- ✓ Almost 50% of teens have been harassed online

- ✓ 71% of children receive messages from strangers online

- ✓ 30% of those children think about meeting those strangers face-to-face

Visit For More Information:
- ✓ www.nobullchallenge.org

- ✓ www.teamnobull.org

Your Checklist:

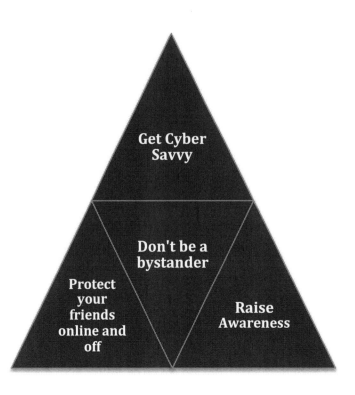

Get Cyber Savvy

Don't be a bystander

Protect your friends online and off

Raise Awareness

Always think before posting/texting
Create an Identity that's you
Privacy Settings & COT
Golden Rule Applies
Blocking on Cell Phones
Blocking on Facebook

Friends DON'T stand by and Watch
"Joining in" is Cyberbullying
Consequences

Don't Forward
Don't Fuel the Fire
Tell a Trusted Adult

Be a Leader instead of a Follower
Start a NO BULL or a FRIENDS ROCK campaign

Tool Kit for Parents & Educators of 10 to 12-year-olds

Online Dangers

Being connected to the digital world is something that isn't going away anytime soon! Having access to technology is just one more way for children and adult predators to target their prey. It's disturbing to know that:

- ✓ About half of all teenagers have experienced some form of online harassment (Cyberbullying Research Center).
- ✓ 37 percent of teens admit to using social networking sites to victimize and harass their peers (TheExaminer.com).
- ✓ 43 percent of teens use their cell phones to say insulting things to others (LG Mobile Phones).
- ✓ 64 percent of all teens say they do things online they don't want their parents to know about (Lenhart, Madden, Rainie, 2006).
- ✓ 71 percent of teens receive messages online from strangers (National Center for Missing and Exploited Children).
- ✓ 51 percent of teens have been asked for personal information online (McAfee Inc.)
- ✓ 83 percent of teens admit to texting in the middle of the night (LG Mobile Phones).
- ✓ 45 percent of teens admit to texting and driving (LG Mobile Phones).
- ✓ 30 percent of teens contemplate meeting a person they met online (Teenage Research Unlimited).
- ✓ 42 percent of youth, age ten to seventeen, have seen Internet porn in the past year. Two-thirds of these exposures were unwanted (University of New Hampshire's Crimes Against Children Research Center).

Be prepared for the worst, it can only get better!

Unlike traditional bullying, anyone is fair game as a target for cyberbullying. While you may think that there is nothing you can do, you are wrong! When it comes to parenting around technology, your first step is to become a defensive parent.

When you were a child, bullies would attack their targets in the schoolyard or parking lot. Now, the cyberbully can torment your child anywhere and anytime. The power of technology gives bullies the ability to reach out to their targets with ease.

Consider This: One of your ex-friends called you a slut on Facebook and posted a picture of you in a bikini she had dug up from a pool party. Within minutes, friends, strangers, and peers had agreed with your new nickname by clicking the "Like" icon or by adding additional comments such as "I agree; she stole my boyfriend!" or "What a loser—she cuts school all the time" or "I heard she does drugs" all within a few hours, and all of this is happening right in front of your eyes. The next day, you have to walk into school with what feels like a scarlet letter tattooed to your forehead. What would you do?

There is no easy answer. Unfortunately, today's youth are finding themselves falling victim to the perils of social and mobile networking hazards at an alarming rate.

According to recent surveys

Humiliation, cyberbullying, textual harassment, sexting, lack of morality, and bad behavior online has become the norm for teens.

- ✓ Over half of bullying and cyberbullying attacks go unreported to parents, educators, or authorities. *
- ✓ On a daily average, 160,000 children miss school because they fear they will be bullied if they attend classes. *
- ✓ On a monthly average, a bully physically attacks 282,000 students each month. *
- ✓ Every seven minutes a child is bullied on a school playground, with over 85 percent of those instances occurring without any intervention. *
- ✓ 50 percent of teens admit to being bullied online or by text message. *
- ✓ As a result of bring bullied, 19,000 children are attempting suicide over the course of one year. *
- ✓ Once every half hour a child commits suicide as a direct result of being bullied. *

* According to the International Adoption Articles Directory

Parents need to open their eyes and realize that it's time to start taking responsibility for what their children are doing online.

The New Schoolyard Bully

Online harassment and cyberbullying is more effective than ever. Bad people can easily connect with their targets hundreds of times a day. Social networks are like virtual stages that online bullies can use to reach out, threaten and harass whenever they choose.

What do you think are the top six reasons that virtual harassment has become the choice of today's bullies are?

1.

2.

3.

4.

5.

6.

How many did you get correct?

The top six reasons virtual harassment has become the choice of today's bullies are:

- ✓ Technology is portable and easy to access
- ✓ It's persistent and instantly harmful
- ✓ Content can be edited and altered
- ✓ It's distributed with lightening speed and breath
- ✓ There is a lack of accountability
- ✓ It's insidious and dangerous

It is not surprising to know that physical fights are a direct result of harassment or threats that originated in the virtual world or by text message. Sometimes, children are harassed and tormented for weeks or months before the physical fight occurs.

Dealing with Cyberbullying

Tips for Parents:

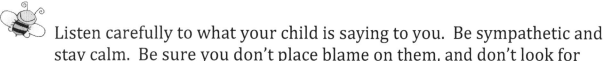

Listen carefully to what your child is saying to you. Be sympathetic and stay calm. Be sure you don't place blame on them, and don't look for fault. Your child needs to know that you understand what is going on and that they can count on you for support.

Teach your child the defensive measures they can take to limit online attack; like: Ignore, Block, Report.

Get professional help if you think your child needs extra support or outside advice.

If your child's safety is at risk, document all of the online and/or text message correspondence, and then contact authorities. Cyberbullying is a serious offense and is taken seriously by authorities.

Keep the lines of communication open with your child and spend extra time with them. Provide extra encouragement whenever possible, and be a friend to your child, as well as a parent.

If you suspect your child is being bullied online while they are at school, contact your child's teacher or the administration of your child's school. But, you will want to try and get your child's approval first. Ask for the school's cooperation in getting cyberbullying to stop.

Always stick to the facts, write them down, and keep copies of everything.

Depending on your child's age and the situation, you might be able to contact the cyberbully's parents for help.

Support and nurture your child's self-confidence levels.

Tell your child not to feel ashamed, that they are not alone, and to reach out to people they can trust for help.

Access to Passwords: Invasion of Privacy or Playing it Safe?

Some parents feel as though they are intruding on their child's privacy if they have access to their social network, cell phone, or email passwords. However, if you implement a safe usage policy at a young age, children will understand that it is a safety precaution, and not so you can know every little detail of their life.

The nature of cyberbullying is discrete and unless you have access to passwords, you as the parent, may never know that it is taking place. Children may share with you some of what is going on, but not to the full extent. Reasons for this include embarrassment, or fear that access to technology will be taken away.

Remember, children these days are digital natives. This means that technology is basically their sole means of communication. If they fear that it will be taken away from them, they will not put their access to technology in jeopardy, even if it means the cyberbullying could stop.

Facts:

- ✓ According to the International Adoption Articles Directory Over half of bullying and cyberbullying attacks go unreported to parents, educators, or authorities.
- ✓ Almost half of our children are harassed using social media
- ✓ 72% of our children receive messages from strangers online

---

Why do you think so many incidents go unreported?

What could you do to make sure your children feel comfortable reporting cyberbullying incidents to you?

Set up username and passwords together	Show them how to network and use the Internet safely
Explain to your child the fun things that the computer is capable of (the good ad the bad)	Take a class with your child so you can both learn something new together

Make it a fun experience

Show your child that you are interested in what they are doing on the computer, and that you want to learn along with them. Many communities offer free computer classes and that could be a wonderful way to open up the communication lines between you and your child. It would also give you an opportunity to learn some of the new applications that have developed since you were a child.

In addition, you could set up a schedule where each member of the family uses the computer around the same time each day. With a schedule in place, it would be very easy to set up chat times with out of town friends and family, and also to show your child that there are positive ways to use technology.

Use this log, or create one of your own to keep all usernames and passwords handy:

Social Network or Webs	Username	Password

Remind your child to NEVER give their passwords out to friends. As an extra precaution, it wouldn't hurt to change the passwords every so often. By doing this, you are preventing some problems from taking place.

Take a few minutes and fill in the chart below.
See if you and your child utilize the computer for
similar reasons.

Parent	Child
What do you like to use the computer for?	What do you like to use the computer for?

Do your answers match up? Most likely not! Parents and children have different agendas when using technology, and that is okay. It is a sign of the times! Children are immersed in technology, and utilize different applications than their parents. However, parents need to be mindful of these differences, and take the initiative on educating themselves about the different applications that their children are interested in.

Many local community centers offer free or low-cost computer courses, which could lend itself to being another bonding experience for you and your child. By immersing yourself in technological applications that your child is familiar with, it may open up another line of communication between you and your child. In addition, it never hurts to be up-to-date on the new technologies that are available. If you show your child early on that you are interested in what they are doing, they may feel more comfortable confronting any issues that are taking place regarding technology.

Once parents/guardians realize that their children have different uses for the computer than they do, it is important to investigate exactly what the child is doing on the computer. I would suggest becoming knowledgeable about the websites that your child frequently visits in addition to learning about the games that are played online and with whom.

I would also encourage having discussions with the parents of your child's friends to see what their policies are at home:

If you send your child to a friend's house, are the same rules and understandings going to be in effect? How are you going to ensure that the expectations that you have set up at home are met at other's homes? If something were to take place at a friend's house, how would you handle the situation? These are all questions that you will want to have answers to. Remember technology is everywhere, so you want to be prepared with how to appropriately handle different situations.

I would recommend engaging in conversation with your child about what they do at other's homes. If they go on the Internet, is someone supervising them?

Brief Description of the Types of Cyberbullying

Impersonation
- When you pretend to be someone else and do mean things while pretending to be that other person. This usually happens on a social network.

Trickery
- You trick someone into believing that you are friends, just so you can find out secrets about that person. You then share all of the secrets with others on a social network or by text.

Exclusion
- You purposely exclude others from what you are doing. This happens frequently in online gaming, in chat rooms, and on social networks.

Harassment and Threats
- You threaten to hurt someone or contiunally bother them with verbal attacks. These can take place on social networks or texts.

Forwarding Embarassing Photos
- You take or find a photo of someone and choose to send it out to everyone in your contact list.

Buzz Words and Phrases

Parents should always be aware of what the buzz is all about, especially when it involves their child and technology. Some buzz words and phrases you will want to keep an ear out for include:

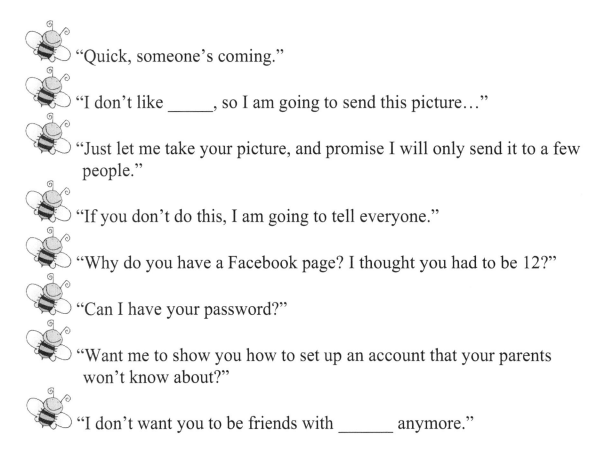

"Quick, someone's coming."

"I don't like _____, so I am going to send this picture…"

"Just let me take your picture, and promise I will only send it to a few people."

"If you don't do this, I am going to tell everyone."

"Why do you have a Facebook page? I thought you had to be 12?"

"Can I have your password?"

"Want me to show you how to set up an account that your parents won't know about?"

"I don't want you to be friends with _____ anymore."

Interest Survey

An interest survey can reveal a lot of important information to both teachers and parents. By finding out what your child's preferences are, it makes it a lot easier to make connections with them, and also plan activities that are also of interest.

1. The main way I communicate with my friends is:

    A. Through e-mail

    B. Through text message

    C. By talking on the phone

    D. Walk over to their house

    E. Other: _____

2. When given the option of working with others, I prefer

    A. Working with one other person

    B. Working in a group

    C. Working by myself

3. My favorite kind of projects are ones that

    A. I get to use technology

    B. I get to draw and handwrite

    C. I get to learn something new from the teacher or classmate

4. If given the option of purchasing technology tools to have in the classroom, or at home, my top few suggestions would be:

A. _____

B. _____

C. _____

D. _____

By reviewing the above answers, it will give you some insight on what technology applications children have been exposed to, and what you need to spend time explaining.

It is always wise for parents to share with teachers the types of technologies that are being used at home, and vice versa. It is best practice for a teacher to send the parents a copy of projects that are completed in school that incorporate technology. This gives the parents a snapshot of what their children are learning at school, and also shows parents how technology is being implemented in the classroom.

By involving parents in the educational process, it demonstrates for the parents how technology is implemented in appropriate ways, and gives them the opportunity to continue what's being learned in school, at home.

Facebook and Other Social Network Rules to Live By

Before allowing your teen to get their Facebook account (or any other social networking site), follow these 10 important Facebook rules to live by:

1. Execute the "Rules of Engagement" with your children.

2. Request their password so you can monitor their online social content and postings on a regular basis. Teach them to safeguard their password. Explain how important it is to not tell anyone their password, not even their best friend.

3. Teach your kids how to use the "Block" and "Report" feature to stop any type of offensive or abusive behavior.

4. Frequently monitor their Facebook pages. Watch for photos, posts, bullies, and anything that doesn't seem right. Watch for "tagging" and photos that have been posted to their profile.

5. Make sure their accounts are always set on "Private" and teach your child to avoid posting private information, especially information that could lead to a physical attack. (Example: address, phone number, etc. should not be posted).

6. Watch out for foul or inappropriate language – have your teen delete posts or updates that include this type of language.

7. Watch out for inappropriate photo posts – teach your children to think twice before posting updates and require your teen to delete inappropriate photos immediately.

8. Require that they only accept friend requests from people they know and frequently review their friend's list, keeping an eye open for people you don't know.

9. Communicate and educate your teens about Internet safety, and how to watch out for online predators. Teach them to trust their instincts; don't carry on conversations with creepy people, and delete them immediately when they come across one.

10. Discuss how "Checking In" or updating a post using Facebook's "Places" is dangerous and off limits.

Important: Facebook and most other social networks require children to be at least 13-years-old before they are allowed to sign up for an account.

Denying Access to Technology

Instead of denying your child access to technology, refer to the contract that you have in place with your child. If the contract states that access will be taken away, then it needs taken away.

By enforcing the guidelines that are set forth in the contract, parents eliminate any misunderstandings of the consequences to breaking the rules.

There is a sample contract for your usage included in the workbook. After referring to it, what additional things would you add to the

Additions to the Contract:

Set Text Boundaries

Because most mobile phones include many bells and whistles like access to the Internet, you'll need to take special precautions by adding a parental control service to your teen's wireless number.

The Buzz reminds you to be aware of the exposure children have to sexting, and to take the following steps to help avoid the risk of sexting from occurring in your family.

We recommend the following tips to help provide peace of mind:

- ✓ For a small monthly fee, all wireless providers offer parental controls
- ✓ Limiting the number of texts sent/received
- ✓ Restricting the times of day the cell phone can be used (great to avoid all of those middle of the night text messages)
- ✓ Restricting online purchases
- ✓ Controlling what number can be blocked from calling or sending/receiving text messages
- ✓ Filtering content/blocking Internet usage

The most important feature of the "parental control" service is that you'll be empowering your child to defend against anyone who is threatening or harassing him or her by text message. Without this service, kids don't have the ability to "block" unwanted callers or texters.

Most importantly, once you've added the service; don't forget to show your kids how to use the block feature with your wireless provider. You'll want to be pro-active about this, so don't wait until they have a problem erupting on text. Instead, add the service, then explain why you've added it and show them exactly how to block unwanted texts.

Text message content monitoring is not usually offered within parental control services due to confidentiality issues. If you feel you need to monitor the content of your child's text messages, you'll need to purchase special software that has text-monitoring capabilities. If you're going to monitor text message content, you *must* tell your child what you are doing and why you're doing it in order to avoid future trust issues.

Resource Guide for Parents & Educators

Shawn Marie Edgington

Shawn is a cyberbullying prevention expert and your go-to cyber safety mom. Shawn's the author of the bestselling book, The Parent's Guide to Texting, Facebook and Social Media: Understanding the Benefits and Dangers of Parenting in a Digital World, the founder of the Cyber Safety Academy and The Great American NO BULL Challenge. She's also the CEO of Granite Insurance Brokers, a national insurance firm, where she provides risk management to clients across the country.

After a personal experience she had with her 16-year-old daughter being physically threatened and stalked by text and on Facebook, Shawn has made it her mission to help parents and teens take the steps necessary to prevent any mobile networking from turning into a one-click nightmare.

Shawn provided her expert advice in Woman's Day Magazine, the upcoming documentary Submit: The Virtual Reality of Cyberbullying, Fox Business, Fox News, View from the Bay, Talk Philly, KRON 4 News, The San Francisco Chronicle, CBS Radio, American Cheerleader Magazine, ESPN Radio, CNN Radio, NPR and various media outlets across the country.

Situations like these happen every day in the news and on the radio, but the majority of them go unreported. What we need are involved parents and solutions that enable them to empower their children to defend against those who harass or bully online or by test message. This book is perfect for the person who wants a roadmap to understanding the benefits and dangers of parenting in a digital world. Knowledge is power; if you're aware of what's happening, you can take action, get involved and facilitate change.

To buy The Parent's Guide, visit Amazon or Barnes & Noble, or anywhere a book is sold. Meet Shawn to learn more about her books and free parent resources at: www.shawnedgington.com. To learn more about how you and your kids can get involved with The Great American NO BULL Challenge, visit: www.nobullchallenge.org.

How You Can Get Involved

Join Team NO BULL

The NO BULL Challenge is the largest, youth-led national campaign against cyberbullying in America's history. We're using the power of social media to inspire 25 million middle and high school students to build each other up, instead of tear each other down.

Everyone will win big just for participating, and finalists will be invited to attend the star-studded NO BULL Teen Video Awards in San Francisco. Inspiring America's teens to stand up and bring an end to cyberbullying, one click at a time, is what The Great American NO BULL Challenge is all about.

Visit **www.nobullchallenge.org** for more infomation on how you can join Team NO BULL!

Start a fundraiser at your school!

Looking for a new way to raise funds for your school, team, church or organization? Tired of offering the same-old fund-raising products that people don't need or want?

The Cyber Safety Academy Fundraising Company offers schools and organizations a new and empowering way to raise funds and awareness about cyber safety and the threat that the virtual world poses to our children.

Visit **www.cybersafetyacademy.com** for more information!

Visit ShawnEdgington.com

We're proud to announce that The Parent's Guide to Texting, Facebook and Social Media: Understanding the Benefits and Dangers of Parenting in a Digital World became an Amazon and a Barnes and Noble bestseller on National Cyber Safety Aware-ness Day. It's a fact that cyberbullying ruins lives.

It's critical that parents take a pro-active approach and become aware of how technology can be abused. When it comes to cyberbullying, knowledge is power, and we're here to help you gain the knowledge that you need!

Visit **www.shawnedgington.com** for more information or visit Amazon to get your copy of The Parent's Guide today.

20219980R00055

Made in the USA
Lexington, KY
25 January 2013